Anonymous

A travelers' directory of the city of Hudson

Containing railroad, steamboat, cab & ferry time tables

Anonymous

A travelers' directory of the city of Hudson
Containing railroad, steamboat, cab & ferry time tables

ISBN/EAN: 9783743467217

Manufactured in Europe, USA, Canada, Australia, Japa

Cover: Foto ©Andreas Hilbeck / pixelio.de

Manufactured and distributed by brebook publishing software
(www.brebook.com)

Anonymous

A travelers' directory of the city of Hudson

"Multum in Parvo."

A

TRAVELERS' DIRECTORY

OF THE

City of Hudson,

CONTAINING

RAILROAD, STEAMBOAT,

Cab & Ferry Time Tables, &c.,

Together with much other miscellaneous information
for the benefit of the public.

H. R. BRYAN, Publisher.

Copyright, 1880.

Wm. Bryan, Printer, Hudson, N. Y.

WM BRYAN.

BOOK

AND

Job Printer,

Republican -Building,

172 Warren Street,

HUDSON, N. Y.

"Multum in Parvo."

A

TRAVELERS' DIRECTORY

OF THE

City of Hudson,

CONTAINING

RAILROAD, STEAMBOAT,

Cab & Ferry Time Tables, &c.,

Together with much other miscellaneous information
for the benefit of the public.

H. R. BRYAN, Publisher.

Wm. Bryan, Printer, Hudson. N. Y.

CALENDAR.

1880.	Sund.	Mon.	Tues.	Wed.	Thur.	Frid.	Sat.
Jan.	..	..	..	..	1	2	3
	4	5	6	7	8	9	10
	11	12	13	14	15	16	17
	18	19	20	21	22	23	24
	25	26	27	28	29	30	31
Feb.	1	2	3	4	5	6	7
	8	9	10	11	12	13	14
	15	16	17	18	19	20	21
	22	23	24	25	26	27	28
	29	..	..	..	..	..	..
Mar	..	1	2	3	4	5	6
	7	8	9	10	11	12	13
	14	15	16	17	18	19	20
	21	22	23	24	25	26	27
	28	29	30	31	..	..	..
Apr.	..	..	..	..	1	2	3
	4	5	6	7	8	9	10
	11	12	13	14	15	16	17
	18	19	20	21	22	23	24
	25	26	27	28	29	30	.
May	..	..	..	..	..	..	1
	2	3	4	5	6	7	8
	9	10	11	12	13	14	15
	16	17	18	19	20	21	22
	23	24	25	26	27	28	29
	30	31	..	..	..	..	..
Jun.	..	..	1	2	3	4	5
	6	7	8	9	10	11	12
	13	14	15	16	17	18	19
	20	21	22	23	24	25	26
	27	28	29	30	..	..	..

1880.	Sund.	Mon	Tues.	Wed.	Thur.	Frid.	Sat
July	..	..	..	..	1	2	3
	4	5	6	7	8	9	10
	11	12	13	14	15	16	17
	18	19	20	21	22	23	24
	25	26	27	28	29	30	31
Aug	1	2	3	4	5	6	7
	8	9	10	11	12	13	14
	15	16	17	18	19	20	21
	22	23	24	25	26	27	28
	29	30	31	..	..	..	..
Sep	..	..	..	1	2	3	4
	5	6	7	8	9	10	11
	12	13	14	15	16	17	18
	19	20	21	22	23	24	25
	26	27	28	29	30	..	..
Oct.	..	..	..	..	..	1	2
	3	4	5	6	7	8	9
	10	11	12	13	14	15	16
	17	18	19	20	21	22	23
	24	25	26	27	28	29	30
	31	..	..	..	..	..	..
Nov	..	1	2	3	4	5	6
	7	8	9	10	11	12	13
	14	15	16	17	18	19	20
	21	22	23	24	25	26	27
	28	29	30	..	..	..	..
Dec	..	..	..	1	2	3	4
	5	6	7	8	9	10	11
	12	13	14	15	16	17	18
	19	20	21	22	23	24	25
	26	27	28	29	30	31	..

Only Remember that

MILO P. MOORE,

Sells Foreign and Domestic

Dry Goods

—AND—

CARPETINGS

**At Old Bottom Prices
Positively.**

HUDSON, N. Y.

Interest Table.
6 PER CENT.

TIME.	$1	$2	$3	$4	$5	$6	$7	$8	$9	$10	$100	$1,000
1 DAY	0	0	0	0	0	0	0	0	0	0	2	17
2 ''	0	0	0	0	0	0	0	0	0	0	3	33
3 ''	0	0	0	0	0	0	0	0	0	1	5	50
4 ''	0	0	0	0	0	0	0	1	1	1	7	67
5 ''	0	0	0	0	0	1	1	1	1	1	8	83
6 ''	0	0	0	0	1	1	1	1	1	1	10	1.00
15 ''	0	1	1	1	1	2	2	2	2	3	25	2.50
2 MO.	1	2	3	4	5	6	7	8	9	10	1.00	10.00
6 ''	3	6	9	12	15	18	21	24	27	30	3.00	30.00
1 YR.	6	12	18	24	30	36	42	48	54	60	6.00	60.00

☞ **Connected by Telephone.** ☜

BYRON PARKER,

Engineer & Machinist,

DEALER IN

PLUMBING, GAS AND STEAM FITTINGS,

236 Warren-st., Hudson.

Table of Wages by the Week.

This Table is based upon Calculation of 10 Hours to a Day.

Wages	1 hour	5 hours	1 day	2 days	3 days	4 days	5 days
$3	.05	.25	.50	1.00	1.50	2.00	2.50
4	$.06\frac{2}{3}$	$.33\frac{1}{3}$	$.66\frac{2}{3}$	$1.33\frac{1}{3}$	2.00	$2.66\frac{2}{3}$	$3.33\frac{1}{3}$
5	$.08\frac{1}{3}$	$.41\frac{2}{3}$	$.83\frac{1}{3}$	$1.66\frac{2}{3}$	2.50	$3.33\frac{1}{3}$	$4.16\frac{2}{3}$
6	.10	.50	1.00	2.00	3.00	4.00	5.00
7	$.11\frac{2}{3}$	$.58\frac{1}{3}$	$1.16\frac{2}{3}$	$2.33\frac{1}{3}$	3.50	$4.66\frac{2}{3}$	$5.83\frac{1}{3}$
8	$.13\frac{1}{3}$	$.66\frac{2}{3}$	$1.33\frac{1}{3}$	$2.66\frac{2}{3}$	4.00	$5.33\frac{1}{3}$	$6.66\frac{2}{3}$
9	.15	.75	1.50	3.00	4.50	6.00	7.50
10	$.16\frac{2}{3}$	$.83\frac{1}{3}$	$1.66\frac{2}{3}$	$3.33\frac{1}{3}$	5.00	$6.66\frac{2}{3}$	$8.33\frac{1}{3}$
11	$.18\frac{1}{3}$	$.91\frac{2}{3}$	$1.83\frac{1}{3}$	$3.66\frac{2}{3}$	5.50	$7.33\frac{1}{3}$	$9.16\frac{2}{3}$
12	.20	1.00	2.00	4.00	6.00	8.00	10.00
14	$.23\frac{1}{3}$	$1.16\frac{2}{3}$	$2.33\frac{1}{3}$	$4.66\frac{2}{3}$	7.00	$9.33\frac{1}{3}$	$11.66\frac{2}{3}$
15	.25	1.25	2.50	5.00	7.50	10.00	12.50
16	$.26\frac{2}{3}$	$1.33\frac{1}{3}$	$2.66\frac{2}{3}$	$5.33\frac{1}{3}$	8.00	$10.66\frac{2}{3}$	$13.33\frac{1}{3}$

F. A. & G. H. MACY,

Dealers in every variety of

Chewing, Smoking and Plug

TOBACCO,

Imported & Domestic Cigars

KINDLING WOOD

by the Cord, Load, Barrel or Bunch.
Agents for DRAIN TILE and

Garnkirk Chimney Tops,

206 WARREN ST.,

HUDSON, N. Y.

DOMESTIC POSTAGE.

On all letters throughout the United States and Canada 3 cts. for each half ounce or fraction thereof if prepaid. Local letters 2 cts. per half ounce where there is a free carrier's delivery ; other offices, 1 ct. Postal Cards 1 cent each.

Money Orders can be sent by mail as follows : Not exceeding $15, 10 cts., $15 to $30, 15 cts., $30 to $40, 20 cts., $40 to $50, 25 cents

Printed Books 1 ct. for each 2 ounces or fraction thereof, not over 4 lbs.

On transient newspapers and other printed matter (including Circulars,) 1 ct. for 2 ounces or part of 2 ounces not over 4 lbs

On Merchandise and and all other articles not calculated to injure the mails, 1 ct for each ounce, not over 4 lbs.

All kinds of Postal Matter may be registered by the payment of a fee of 10 cts. in addition to the regular postage

All transient matter must be fully prepaid by stamps. All matter except Letters, must be so inclosed that a free inspection is allowed, without cutting strings or wrapper.

ESTALISHED 1860.

JEAN BACH,

PRACTICAL

WATCHMAKER, JEWELER

AND DEALER IN

Watches, Fine Jewelry, Silver and Plated
Ware, Clocks, Bronzes, Fancy
Optical Goods, Cutlery
etc., etc.,

Offers his friends this season an immense
variety of fine goods, Gold Watches, Cameo
Sets, Band Bracelets in Etruscan, Chased
and Enameled, and all other articles gen-
erally found in a first-class Jewelry Estab
lishment Special attention is called to
the fine display of Wedding and Holiday
Presentation pieces at moderate prices.

Watch Repairing a Specialty.

Engraving done in the store. Eyes fit-
ted in the best and most approved manner.

205 Warren Street.

FOREIGN POSTAGE.

To all parts of Europe, British India, Newfoundland, Brazil, Mexico, &c , Letters, 5 cts. per half oz., prepayment optional ; if not prepaid, a fine is collected on delivery. Postal Cards, 2 cts. each. Newspapers, 2 cents each, if not over 4 ounces, and 2 cents for each additional 4 ounces or part thereof For other printed matter and samples 1 ct. for each 2 ounces or fraction thereof—the *minimum* rate for *commercial* papers being 5 cts , and for samples 2 cts. All matter except Letters, must be at least partially prepaid. Letters and other packages may be registered on payment of a fee of 10 cts. The fees for Money Orders on Great Britain and Ire land and Switzerland are not over $10, 25 cts.; $10 to $20, 50 cts.; $20 to $30, 75 cts ; $30 to $40, $1 ; $40 to $50, $1.25. On Germany, not over $5, 15 cts ; $5 to $10, 25 cts ; $10 to $20, 50.cts ; $20 to $30, 75 cts.; $30 to $40, $1 ; $40 to $50, $1 25

Postage to the Dominion of Canada, New Brunswick, Nova Scotia,&c., same as U. S. rates

LONDON AND LANCASHIRE

Fire Insurance Co.

United States Branch Statement.
January 1, 1880.

Total Assets............... .. $775,003.10
Total Liabilities................ 308,063.73

Net Surplus over all Liabilities $466,939.37

Income in 1879

Premiums Received........... $421,354.55
Interest and other sources.... 4,223.78

Total Income in U. S.......... $425,578 33

Expenditures in 1879.

Losses Paid..................... $103,848.70
All other items................ 108,588 91

$212,437.61

Excess of Income over expenditures in the 6 months during which the Company has been established in this Country............ .... $213,140.72

A. P PITCHER, Agent,
327 Warren-st., Hudson, N. Y.
Represents 6 other Companies.

CITY GOVERNMENT.

Mayor—Joshua T. Waterman.
Recorder—Albert Hoysradt.

ALDERMEN.

First Ward—David Barry, Daniel Mc-Carthy.

Second Ward—George Millard, John E. Heath.

Third Ward—Peter A. Brusie, Samuel G. Rowles.

Fourth Ward—Henry James, Stephen W. Ham.

Clerk—Gardner C. McArthur.
Messenger—Frank Price.
City Treasurer—Elihu Gifford, Jr.
Police Justice—John M. Welch.
Chief Police—Almon Snyder.
Health Officer—Crawford E. Fritts.
Justice of Peace—W. F. Holsapple.

COUNTY OFFICERS—1880.

County Judge ....H. W. McClellan.
Surrogate...... ....Isaac N. Collier.
County Clerk.............Chas. Whitbeck.
District Attorney... ......John B. Longley.
Sheriff.................Chester Miller.
Under Sheriff............Walter Shutts.
County Treasurer. ......C. W. Hinsdale.
Superintendent of Poor. Philip Niver.
*Sup't of Pub. Buildings.*Ezra A. Traver.
School Com'r, 1st *Dist*...Amasa P. Lasher.
    "   2d *Dist*...Geo V. Bushnell.
Loan Commissioner. ......Cyrus Groat.
    "   "   ......
Justice of Sessions........H. P. VanHosen.
    "   "   ......Nich. Robison.
Coroner............. ....W. M Holsapple
    "   ....W. W. Rogers.
    "   ....Erskine Waldron.
    "   ....B. A Weeks.

LEGISLATIVE OFFICERS.

Member of Congress......J. H. Ketcham.
Senator........ ....S H. Wendover.
Assemblyman...... ....John E. Gillette..

For Board of Supervisers see page 44.

Public Buildings and Offices.

City Hall—corner Warren street and City Hall place. Contains Mayor's and City Clerk's offices, Police Headquarters and Court Room and Common Council room.

Court House—south end 4th street. Contains Sheriff's and County Clerk's offices, County Court room, etc

Hudson Water Works—Pumping house at river, west of H. R. R. Reservoir Prospect Hill, head of Warren street.

Col. Co. Surrogate's office—300 Warren street.

District Attorney's office—208 Warren street.

County Treasurer's office—180 Warren street.

City Treasurer's office—147 Warren st

BANKS.

FARMERS' NATIONAL BANK—302 Waren st. J. W. Hoysradt, President ; Chas C. Macy, Cashier.

FIRST NATIONAL BANK—City Hall. R. B. Shepard, President ; Wm. Seymour, Cashier.

NATIONAL HUDSON RIVER BANK—99 Warren-st. Ezra Waterbury, President ; Wm. Bostwick, Cashier.

HUDSON CITY SAVINGS BANK—98 Warren-st. Henry J. Baringer, President ; Edwin C. Terry, Sec. and Treas.

NEWSPAPERS.

HUDSON DAILY REPUBLICAN–Published every morning, Sunday excepted. Wm. Bryan, ed. and prop , 172 Warren-st.

HUDSON EVENING REGISTER–Published every evening, Sunday excepted. M. Parker Williams, ed. and prop., Central Square.

COLUMBIA REPUBLICAN AND HUDSON WEEKLY STAR–Published every Thursday. Wm. Bryan, ed. and prop,, 172 Warren-st.

HUDSON GAZETTE—Published every Thursday. M. Parker Williams, ed. and prop., Central Square.

Oakley & Elkenburgh,

DEALERS IN

GROCERIES,

PROVISIONS,

Foreign and Domestic

FRUITS,

262 Warren St.,

HUDSON, N. Y.

Western Union Tel. Co.

Office, No. 192 Warren street. Open from 8 A. M. to 8 P. M.

Office at H. R. R. depot. Open day and night.

American Union Tel. Co.

Office, No. 173 Warren street. Open from 8 A. M. to 8 P. M.

Hudson Telegraph and Telephone Co.

Office, No. 171 Warren street. Open day and night. Messenger service connected.

H. C. TURNER,

DEALER IN

Millinery

AND

FANCY GOODS.

HARRIS KID GLOVES.

No. 279 Warren Street,

HUDSON, N. Y.

American Express Co.

Office, No. 107 Warren street. Express closes :

Going North—7.45 A. M., 2.45 and 6.30 P. M.

Going South—2.45, 6.30 and 8.00 P. M.

Money sent at the following rates : Not exceeding $20.00, 15 cents ; not exceeding $40.00, 20 cents ; not exceeding $50.00, 25 cents.

Large sums in much smaller proportion.

Books and other printed matter, if pre-paid, as follows : 2 lbs., 15 cents ; 3 lbs., 20 cents ; 4 lbs., 25 cents.

Orders for purchasing goods left with any agent of the Company will be executed without other expense than the ordinary charge for carrying the goods.

THE BEST

BRANDS OF CHOICE IMPORTED

Cigars and

Cigarettes,

FROM PARK & TILFORD'S,

kept constantly on hand at

WILLIAM VAN BECK'S

Hair Dressing Rooms,

NO. 145 WARREN ST.,

HUDSON, N. Y.

N. Y. C. & H. R. R. R.

Hudson Station.

DEPOT SOUTH END FRONT STREET.

GOING NORTH.

*5:03 A. M.—Night Express. Leaves N. Y. 11.00 Arrives at Albany 6.30.

7:43 A. M.—Alb. Local. LEAVES Po'keepsie 6.10. ARRIVES at Alb. 8.55.

12:01 P. M.—Chicago Ex. LEAVES N. Y. 8.00. Arrives at Alb. 1.00.

1:58 P M.—Special Chicago Ex. Leaves N. Y. 10.30. Arrives at Alb. 2.50

3:14 P. M.—North and Western Ex. Leaves N. Y. 11.03. Arrives at Alb. 4 15.

6:59 P. M.—Saratoga Special Leaves N.Y. 3.30. Arrives at Albany 7.45

8:08 P. M.—Troy Express. Leaves N. Y. 4 00. Arrives at Albany 9 15.

*9:24 P M.—St. Louis Pacific Ex. Leaves N. Y. 6.00. Arrives at Alb. 10.15.

*Run also on SUNDAY.

SCHENCK & TURNER,

GENERAL

Life and Fire

INSURANCE AGENTS,

201 and 203 WARREN STREET,

[Odd Fellows Temple,]

HUDSON, N. Y.

We represent the Very Best Foreign and American Companies in the World.

Assets................. ....$46,723,368.52
Net surplus over all liabilities   8,710,453.34

Give us a call and see what we can do for you in the way of rates. Orders by mail or telegraph promptly attended to.

N. Y. C. & H. R. R. R.

Hudson Station.

DEPOT SOUTH END OF FRONT ST.

GOING SOUTH.

*7:19 A: M.—St. L. Ex. LEAVES Alb. 6.30. ARRIVES at N Y: 10.30.

6:51 A. M.—Local Exp. Leaves Alb. 5.50. Arrives at N. Y. 11.05.

10:55 A M.—Saratoga Special. Leaves Troy 9.50. Arrives at N. Y, 2 20

11:32 A. M.—Local Ex. Leaves Alb. at 10 20. Arrives at N. Y. 3.45

3:14 P. M.—Alb, Local. Leaves Alb. 2.15. Arrives at N. Y. 7.48.

3:35 P. M.—Special N. Y. Ex. Leaves Alb. 2.40. Arrives at N. Y. 7.00

*6:32 P. M.—Limited Ex. Leaves Alb 5.40. Arrives at N. Y. 10.00.

*7:06 P. M.—Milk and Passenger. Leaves Alb 5 45. Arrives at N. Y. 1 30.

11:27 P. M.—Night Ex. Leaves Troy 9.30. Arrives at N. Y. 5.30 A. M.

*Run also on SUNDAY.

TIME TABLE
Hudson & Chat. Branch B. & A. R. R.
HUDSON TO CHATHAM.

LEAVE.	1st Passen-ger.	2d Passen-ger.	3d Passen-ger.	4th Passen-ger
Hudson.....	6 25am	9.40am	2.15PM	5.25PM
Hudson Upper	6.40	9.55	2.25	5 40
Claverack ..	6.51	10.05	2.34	5.51
Mellenville	7.04	10.18	2.47	6.04
Pulvers.....	7.11	10.25	2.54	6.11
Ghent.......	7.24	10.38	3.07	6.24
Chatham ...	7.32	10.46	3.15	6.32

CHATHAM TO HUDSON.

LEAVE.	1st Passenger	2d Passenger	3d Passenger	4th Passenger
Chatham ...	9 06am	12.10PM	2.20PM	5.10PM
Ghent.......	9.14	12.20	2.28	5.18
Pulvers.....	9.25	12.33	2.39	5.31
Mellenville	9.33	12.41	2.47	5.38
Claverack..	9.46	12.55	2.59	5.51
Hudson Upper	9.55	1.05	3.07	6.00
Hudson.....	10.06	1 15	3.17	6.10

Depots head State St. and at H. R. R. Depot, south end of Front Street.
☞Trains run on Boston time.

CHATHAM CONNECTIONS
WITH
HUDSON & CHATHAM BRANCH
OF BOSTON & ALBANY R. R.

Boston and Albany.

Going East, leave Chatham at 2.53, 7.48 and 10.56 A. M.; 4.05, 5.56 and 6.34 P. M.

Going West, at 12.39 and 9.06 A. M.; 12.10, 2.20, 5.10 and 9.31 P. M.

New York and Harlem.

Leave Chatham, 6.05 A. M, and 4.10 P. M.

Arrive at New York, 10.45 A. M., and 8.55 P. M.

Leave New York, 10.30 A. M., and 3.50 P. M.

Arrive at Chatham, 3.10 and 8.45 P. M.

Harlem Extension.

Trains arrive at Chatham Village at 8.25 A. M., and 3.22 P. M.

Trains leave Chatham Village at 9.15 A. M., and 4.00 P. M.

₹ STEAMERS

McMANUS AND REDFIELD

Leave Hudson from wharf south of Ferry Slip every night except Saturday at 7 P. M., and New York from Pier 35 every night except Sunday, at 6 P. M.

Day Line—New York and Albany.

Steamers C. VIBBARD & ALBANY.

GOING NORTH

Brooklyn (by annex) leave......	8.00	A. M.
N. Y., Vestry street............	8.35	"
" 24th street............	9.00	"
HUDSON...................	3.45	P. M.
Albany (arrive)............	6.10	"

GOING SOUTH.

Albany	8.30	A. M.
HUDSON...................	10.40	"
N. Y. 24th street............	5.30	P. M.
" Vestry street............	5.50	"
Brooklyn (by annex) arrive......	6.20	"

Dock north side of Ferry Slip.

Fancy Goods.

W. C. FALK,

301 WARREN ST.

HUDSON. N. Y.

Men's Furnisher.

DAILY LINE
Newburgh, Hudson and Albany.

Steamers EAGLE and M. MARTIN.

Dock north side of Ferry Slip.

TIME TABLE, 1880.
Going North.

Leave Newburgh..................	7.00 A M.
" Hudson........	1.15 P. M.
Arrive Albany....................	4.00 "

Going South.

Leave Albany...	7.30 A. M.
" Hudson......	10 15 "
Arrive Newburgh................	4.30 P M

Daily Line Catskill & Albany
Steamer City of Hudson.

Leaves Catskill 6.30 ; HUDSON 7.00 ; Arrives Albany 10.00.

Returning leaves Albany 3.00 P. M ; leaves HUDSON 6.00 P. M., ; Arrives at Catskill 6.30.   Landing both ways at Coxcackie, Stuyvesant, New Baltimore, Coeymans, Castleton, Cedar Hill.

Dock north side of Ferry Slip.

Sign of the American Flag

HUTCHING'S

Dining Rooms,

Meals at all hours of the day.

Fine Confectionery,

Fruits, Foreign and Domestic Cigars
and ICE CREAM in large
quantities a Specialty.

295 WARREN STREET.

ATHENS AND HUDSON.
FERRY-BOAT GEO. H. POWER.
Time Table, June, 1880.

SUNDAY TRIPS. A. M.—6.00, 7 00, 8.20, 9.00, 10.00, 11.00, 11.45. P. M.–1.30, 2.00, 2.45, 3.25, 4.10, 4.50, 6.00, 6.40, 7.20.	Leave Athens.	Leave Hudson.	SUNDAY TRIPS' A M—6.15, 7.30, 8.40, 9.30, 10.30, 11.20, 12.15. P M—1.45, 2 25, 3.05, 3.50, 4 30, 5 10, 6.20, 7.10, 7.35,
	5.30 A. M.	5.45 A. M	
	6.30 "	6.40 "	
	7.00 "	7.10 "	
	7 25 "	7.50 "	
	8.25 "	8.45 "	
	9.00 "	9.20 "	
	9.40 "	10.00 "	
	10.25 "	10.45 "	
	11.00 "	11.15 "	
	11.30 "	12.05 P. M.	
	1.00 P. M.	1.20 "	
	1.40 "	2.00 "	
	2.20 "	2.35 "	
	2.50 "	3.15 "	
	3.35 "	3.50 "	
	4.10 "	4.30 "	
	4.50 "	5.00 "	
	5.30 "	5.40 "	
	6.00 "	6.25 ".	
	6 40 "	7.10 "	
	7.45 "	8.10 "	

HUDSON
CAB LINE.
TIME TABLE.
Fare 10 Cents.

Leave head Warren Street at		*Leave Franklin Sq., at the River, at*	
6:35 A M	2:00 P M	6:55 A M	2:00 P M
7:00	2:25	7:25	2:25
7:20	2:50	7:50	2:50
8:05	3:15	8:30	3:15
8:25	3:45	9:00	3:45
9:00	4:15	9:30	4:15
9:30	4:40	10:00	4:40
10:00	5:45	10:30	5:00
10:30	6:05	11:00	6:10
11:00	6:35	11:20	6:25
11:30	6:50	12:05 P M	7:00
12:45 P M	7:30	1:10	7:15
1:15	7:40	1:35	8:10
1:35			

CLUB STABLES,

. Diamond Street,

(Between 5th and 6th.)

LIVERY, SALE

and Exchange.

A fine assortment of Side Bar Wagons, Phaetons, &c , constantly on hand, at New York prices. Before purchasing your

Fancy Teams and Work Horses,

call and examine our stock.

In our LIVERY DEPARTMENT can be found the *Finest Turnouts in the County.*

Double or Single Rigs can be ordered by Telephone.

Steam Yacht Bessie,

DOCK SOUTH SIDE FERRY SLIP.

Leaves Hudson daily at 8:20 A. M., 1:20 P. M. and 4:20 P. M.

Leaves Catskill daily at 11:00 A. M , 3:00 P. M. and 6:00.

SUNDAY TIME TABLE.

Leaves Hudson at 8:20 A. M., 1:50 P. M. and 5:15 P. M.

Leaves Catskill at 10:30 A. M , 3:00 P. M. and 6:30 P. M.

☞ Lands at Hamburgh and N. Y. City Ice Company's dock if requested.

STAGE LINES.

Stage leaves Post Office for Stottville, Stockport, Stuyvesant Falls and Kinderhook at 8 A. M., arrives at Kinderhook, 10:30 A. M. Returning, leaves Kinderhook 1:30 P. M., arrives at Hudson 4 P. M.

Stages leave P. O. for Humphreyville, Livingston, Blue Store and Clermont at 1 P. M.

Hudson Post Office,

CITY HALL BUILDING

MAILS ARRIVE.

New York... ....7:00 a. m , 12.30 p m.
South Way ......   7:45 a. m., 12:30 p. m.
Rhine k & Ct. R.R. Po'k'sie & Kingston 7:00 a.m.
Albany......7:45 a. m., 12:30, 4:00 and 7:00 p. m.
North Way   ... .7:45 a. m . 12:30 and 4 p. m.
Troy .. ..7:45 a m., 12:30, 4 and 7 p. m.
Athens...................................7:45 a. m.
Claver'k & Chatham Village,10:15 a.m., 6:15 p.m.
Boxton & Albany R. R................1:30 p. m.
Kinderhook & Stoitville....   ....4:30 p. m.
Harlem R.R.. Mellenville and Ghent .6:15 p. m.
Livingston & Taghkanic.... ...Daily at 10 a m.

MAILS CLOSE.

N Y. & Po'k'psie, 6:50 11 a. m.. 3, 5:50, 7:30 p. m
South Way..............6:50, 11 a. m. and 3 p. m.
Albany and West..............11 a.m., 7:30 p. m.
Troy .... .11 a.m., 7:30 p. m.
Rhinebeck & Ct. R.R..................6:50 a. m.
Claver'k and Chatham Village..... 2 and 8 p. m.
Athens........ ....6:50 a. m.
Harlem Railroad and Ghent, ...2 p m.
B & A. R.R.. Ghent and Mellenville....8 p. m.
Kinderhook & Stottville....., ...8 a. m,
Livingston and Taghkanic .Daily at 12:45 p. m.
Western States...... .... 11 a. m., 3 and 7:30 p. m.

Board of Supervisors.

COLUMBIA COUNTY.

Chairman—M. L. Bates.
Clerk—Ruluf Neefus.
Supervisors—Jacob Miller, Ancram ; C. Gamwell Varney, Austerlitz; M. L. Bates, Canaan ; John J. Wilbor, Chatham ; Henry P. Horton, Claverack ; Wm. H. Rockefeller, Clermont ; William Dinehart, Copake ; George Younghanse, Gallatin ; Philip W. Rockefeller, Germantown ; Martin V. Stupplebeen, Ghent ; Frederick W. Jones, Greenport ; Lorenzo Gilbert, Hillsdale ; James Kane, 1st Ward, Hudson ; Matthew Kennedy, 2d Ward ; Levi P. Couse, 3d Ward ; Conklin W. Oakley, 4th Ward ; Jeremiah B. Richmond, Kinderhook ; James W. Ham, Livingston ; Franklin Hand, New Lebanon ; Henry S. Van DeCarr, Stockport ; A. L. Schermerhorn, Stuyvesant ; John NcNeal, Taghkanic.

A. BEHRENS,

Harness Maker

—AND—

Carriage Trimmer,

DEALER IN

TRUNKS, VALISES, &c.,

167 Warren-st.,

HUDSON, N. Y.

Official Paper of City.

HUDSON REPUBLICAN,

(DAILY,)

Published every morning, (Sundays excepted.)

SUBSCRIPTION $7 PER YEAR
in advance.

COLUMBIA REPUBLICAN,

(WEEKLY.)

PUBLISHED EVERY THURSDAY.

Subscription $1.50 per year in advance

Official Paper of County

www.ingramcontent.com/pod-product-compliance
Lightning Source LLC
Chambersburg PA
CBHW022040080426
42733CB00007B/919